Rebuilt

Rebuilt
No Limitations, Just Possibilities

Ephrom Levi Lafleur

REBUILT
NO LIMITATIONS, JUST POSSIBILITIES

Scripture quotations marked AMP are from The Amplified Bible, Old Testament copyright © 1965, 1987 by the Zondervan Corporation. The Amplified Bible, New Testament copyright © 1954, 1958, 1987 by The Lockman Foundation. Used by permission. All rights reserved.

Scripture quotations marked NIV are taken from the Holy Bible, New International Version®. NIV®. Copyright © 1973, 1978, 1984 by International Bible Society. Used by permission of Zondervan. All rights reserved. [Biblica]

iUniverse books may be ordered through booksellers or by contacting:

iUniverse
1663 Liberty Drive
Bloomington, IN 47403
www.iuniverse.com
844-349-9409

Because of the dynamic nature of the Internet, any web addresses or links contained in this book may have changed since publication and may no longer be valid. The views expressed in this work are solely those of the author and do not necessarily reflect the views of the publisher, and the publisher hereby disclaims any responsibility for them.

Any people depicted in stock imagery provided by Getty Images are models, and such images are being used for illustrative purposes only. Certain stock imagery © Getty Images.

ISBN: 978-1-6632-1030-2 (sc)
ISBN: 978-1-6632-1031-9 (e)

Library of Congress Control Number: 2021901661

Print information available on the last page.

iUniverse rev. date: 02/01/2021

I thank God for his inspiration to write this book and for seeing it accomplish what it was meant to do—inspire others.

A Knock at My Door

Behold, I stand at the door [of the church] and continually knock. If anyone hears My voice and opens the door, I will come in and eat with him (restore him), and he with Me.

—Revelation 3:20 (AMP)

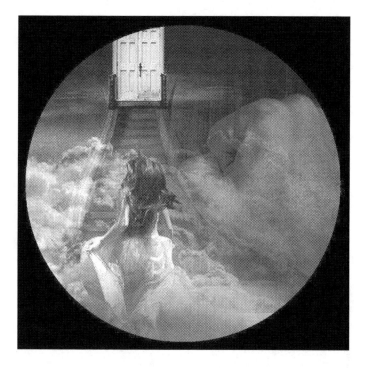

My eyes were closed to what was in front of me.

Things I despised seeing in society have now become a part of me.

A man without a vision or a plan,

Just got lost in No Man's Land.

Sins, how could this be?
Falling into traps and blaming society.
A look in the mirror, and I still could not see
That person who had a vision of becoming somebody.

My friends and family never encouraged me.
In fact, they did the opposite and shuttered the positive me.
It was my fault to entertain those things in my brain,
Never letting go of the hurt and the pain.
I meditated on them day and night,
Not lifting my voice to put up a fight.

Then there was a knock on my door.
A voice asked, "May I come in to explore and restore?

"I have watched you for many years.
My heart was filled with so many tears
From the teaching and preaching you have heard.
You have gone against all my words.

You had struggles that held you back,
That kept you from walking toward the right path.
A drink here, a drink there.
No matter what drink came, you simply didn't care.
Yes, you did take a puff or two.
That was so you could look good and feel cool.

Having a sexual partner every other day,

Two days were too long for them to ever stay.

"Your eyes were closed to what was in front of you.

Couldn't see your sins were overpowering you.

I had placed you in a secure place,

So the enemy wouldn't be able to shake your faith.

But you stepped out on your own,

Moved too quickly; yes, you moved too soon.

You used the world's system, and you are surprised

You had such a miserable life.

The things you did I did not ordain,

So the pain and misery came with the things you entertained."

There was a knock at my door.

I answered and said yes to the Lord,

He could come in to explore and restore.

Let's Talk

Have you ever been faced with many stressful situations that you couldn't figure out? Be honest. Please be honest with yourself.

Have you ever just opened your mouth and said, "Lord, I don't know what to do"? That statement is a sign of surrender. Knowingly or unknowingly, it's a simple prayer asking God for help. God summons his angels and says, "My child is in need of my help. Go assist." Maybe someone, a familiar person or a stranger, comes out of the blue. Maybe you hear a song that seems to be speaking to you, or a TV show features a similar situation with a positive outcome. In truth, it is God knocking, trying to get the answers or results to us.

Let me put it like this, without taking up too much of your time. It is a knock at your door. God is trying to establish a relationship with us. He isn't going to force himself on us; he wants us to invite him in. He wants to give us a secure life, a peaceful life, a joyful life, a productive life, a life that will help others who are broken, a life filled with wisdom to know how to deal with situations when they arrive. But we must answer when he knocks, which is every day.

If we push our situations aside, listen carefully, and pay attention, we will receive all that he has for us.

I know you have what it takes to make the right choice. You will do well. Thanks for answering.

A Realized Dream

Commit your work to the Lord, and
your plans will be established.

—Proverbs 16:3

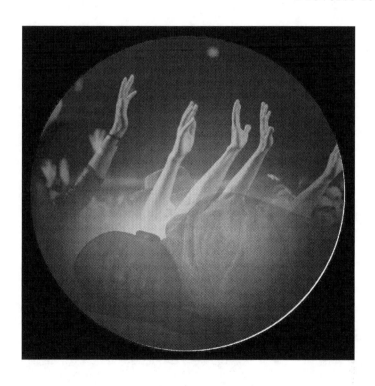

I had a dream of who I was intended to be,

A dream above a level I thought was impossible to reach.

I tried and tried with all my might

Not to forget my dream this particular night.

It was revealed to me who I am supposed to be.

But I opened my eyes and faced reality—

That my surroundings and situations were keeping me down,

That the dream I saw seemed as if it would never be found.

Lying in a bed of extreme sin,

This was a battle I had to win.

No other addiction could ever stop me

From becoming who God predestined me to be.

But this one had taken me by the hand

And led me to a place I could no longer stand.

I was sinking; yes, I was sinking fast.

Then I remembered a powerful word from my past.

Jesus, Jesus, Jesus, Jesus. (The word)

Lord, thank you for allowing me to be able to call on you in my time of need.

Lord, life situations are heavy on my back.

These addictions are constantly on the attack,

Keeping me from walking on the right path.

It seems these situations will always last.

Oh, my Lord, help me, please.

These storms of life are slowly destroying me.

I read the Bible a day or two and remembered what it

Said you can do.

You are faithful and just to forgive.

You have the power of forgiving me for all that I did.

You also said to confess my sins,

So I told you all that was buried deep within.

Your Word also said to accept Jesus Christ as Lord and Savior,

So I gave it all to you; I surrendered my all just to you.

I also asked to be baptized in Jesus's name

So I can be reborn and be made clean.

I had a dream of who I was destined to be,

A man or woman going towards God's plans for me

I Am Turning My Knob

It is done unto you as you believe.

—Matthew 9:29

I am turning; I am turning, yes indeed,
I am turning the knob of life,
Going toward my dreams.
Low self-esteem, you hindered me long enough.
Took me for garbage, kicked me around; now enough is enough.

I am turning; I am turning, yes indeed,
I am turning the knob of life,
Going toward my dreams.
A crack in the door, thank you, Lord.
This is the moment I have been waiting for.

I will push hard with all my might.
I see this is the moment for me to stand and fight.
My hopes and dreams depend on this
For my life has been one big mess.
One door open; yes, I see a few more to be opened.
What do I do?

Pray, pray, pray.
Thank you, Lord, for your protection, your provision, your guidance,
Your wisdom and your favor.
Thank you for opening doors that no man can close
And closing doors no man can open.
Father, I know you have prepared me for such a time as this
To walk through the doors that you personally have picked.

I may sometimes feel unworthy of the blessings and favors you have poured upon me due to the sinful Nature that was born within me.

Thank you for forgiving me of all the wrong I have done

And for showing me that I am still your son.

In the name of Jesus I pray. Amen.

I am turning; I am turning, yes indeed,

I am turning the knob of life,

Going toward my dreams.

I stand on you, oh, Lord,

To be my strength while walking through those doors.

Destroy, destroy is what the enemy sends after me,

Never wanting me to walk into my destiny.

But the hands of the Lord, so mighty and pure,

Have given me the strength to walk through the open doors.

I have turned my knob, not to sneak a peak,

But to walk the path of life the Lord has chosen for me.

With my head held high and my faith restored,

I have stepped through my first opened door.

Tell me, when will you open yours?

God Knows Why

---•◦◦◦•---

For I know the thoughts I think towards you,
says the Lord, thoughts of peace and not of
evil, to give you a future and a hope.

—Jeremiah 29:11

It was a Thursday morning, around ten o'clock.

I remember having a conversation with a wonderful woman of God.

For a moment she was burdened by something she had

carried on her chest for years.

She began to weep, asking, "Why did this happen? Why, Lord, why?"

I was lost for words because I had never seen her in this state.

Questions ran through my mind:

What happened? What triggered this emotional breakdown?

All I knew was she was cleaning the front glass of the church,

so I ran to look by the front glass.

Honestly, I thought she might have seen her husband with another woman.

But it wasn't so.

I caught a glimpse of a man and a woman pushing a baby stroller; that was all.

"God knows why we go through situations and losses; everything happens for a reason," I replied.

She turned to me, and with a painful look said,

"I have lost two babies for my husband.

Yes, two miscarriages.

It pains me not to be able to give my husband a child."

Shocked by the conversation I was being pulled into,

I asked the Holy Spirit in my heart to take the lead in this conversation,

Giving me the words to comfort my sister's grieving heart.

The first thing I said was,

"God knows why we go through situations and losses; everything happens for a reason."

"What do you mean?" she asked.

My reply through the Holy Spirit,

"Something needed to be fixed before the Father would allow a

Child to be brought into your life."

She said, "Thanks," and a peaceful look appeared on her face.

I didn't understand her response; it wasn't my place to understand.

I was just meant to be led by the Holy Spirit.

She said, "Pray for my husband. Could you do that for me?

My husband used to abuse me [keywords "used to," past tense] verbally and physically.

He broke me down in our early years of marriage

with his countless affairs, name-calling, drinking, gambling, etc. [anything negative].

It drove me to have suicidal thoughts, low self-esteem, depression.

Pressure was always high; my weight went from a sexy size 6 to a size 18.

I was a broken vessel for the Lord."

"God knows why we go through situations and losses; everything happens for a reason."

"Thank God for placing people in our lives who prayed for us and who helped us

with our emotional and spiritual struggles. Thank God for the brothers in church and the pastor who counseled my husband. And I must add they did not judge my husband for all that

he did nor held it against him.

My husband and I now attend church services together. We got baptized in Jesus's name. We lead the kids' ministry, and by doing so, we are filling that void of not having our own children until the Lord feels it time for our own. We continue to pray and hold faith that we will receive our own."

"God knows why we go through situations and losses; everything happens for a reason."

It made sense now!

Our father is a God of order; He removes things from us so he can

place us in a better location and situation. We lean too much on our own understanding, trying to figure out why this and that has happened to us. Not knowing that God is trying to get "The Promise" to us that we may be prosperous in every area of our lives.

Points

If she did have the baby, what type of environment would the baby be placed in?

What other pressures would have been added to her stressful life?

This list can go on and on; let us not focus on what took place but let us seek God for guidance and understanding.

Read about Joseph's life in the Genesis 37–50, and you would have a greater understanding about, "God knows why we go through situations and losses; everything happens for a reason." The process may be hard, but if you let go and let God, there is a rewarding life.

I Stand

I can do all things through Him who strengthens me.

—Philippians 4:13

I stand with a divine plan not of man
But that of the Master mind
I am a weak man, that I must admit, but
With the strength of the Lord, I will never quit.

Situations will come but not get the best of me
Because I am equipped with God's plans and His big strategies.
I will praise the Lord all my days.
While the storms of life try to blow my talents and dreams away,
I will continue to pray through the storm.
Equipped with the armor of the Lord,
My God will make sure I am secure.

So no more running away or slipping with disgrace.
The Lord has helped me to win this race.
No more being kicked down and pushed around.
My God has me positioned on solid ground.

I stand with grace and a smile on my face,
Knowing that the Lord removed all my bad traits.
No more of this, no more of that.
The Lord has me going on the right track.
I stand in amazement because of You.
I know what You have brought me through.
I stand, I stand with the Master's plan
To fulfill my destiny that my God has commanded.

Looking by Faith

In peace I will lie down and sleep, for you alone, Lord, make me dwell in safety.

—Psalm 4:8 (AMP)

I am looking but can't see.
I am looking, but I can't believe
That what I have worked so hard for
Has no value to its name.
How could this be?
The life I want, which is just in front of me,
Doesn't seem as if it will become a reality.

Problems, problems, stress, stress.
Life has placed a heavy burden on my chest.

I am looking, but I can't see.
I am looking, but I am starting to sink.
Rent and bills are dragging me down.
Everywhere I look, expenses are always around.
So I go to a fantasyland,
Where I have everything I possibly can.
A fantasy world with house and cars,
With a cash flow that was made to last.

Words from a Pastor:
"Wake up, wake up; open your eyes
So you can see
That everything you dreamed about
Can become a reality.

"Do you pray?

Do you read the Word (Bible)?

Do you go to church?

But most of all,

Do you believe and trust in God?

Those questions played a role in my life,

To let me know everything is possible through Jesus Christ.

You can dream dreams,

But without God, you can't accomplish anything.

He is the One who gives you the strength

And the ability to endure.

When the rent man comes knocking at your door,

He makes a way when you can't see

That your bills can be paid based on his strategies.

"The Word covers us as we go through our days,

Leading and guiding while protecting us along the way.

The church allows you to understand

The will and purpose of the Master's plans.

The preaching and teaching will help

Pull you through

When you 'think' you're sinking,

And you don't know what to do.

"When you begin to trust in God,

He has the power to restore

The things you've lost and the things you saw.

His power will help comfort you

While assuring you about what He is able to do."

I am looking; yes, I can now see

My future life can be a reality.

I am looking, I am looking, but this time I am looking with faith.

Lost Chance

For lack of discipline they will die, led
astray by their own great folly.

—Proverbs 5:23 (NIV)

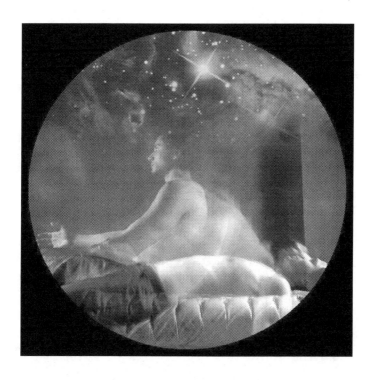

I awoke this morning, got on my knees, and prayed,

Thanking the Lord for waking me up to see another day.

I walked to the kitchen to find something to eat.

Said good morning to everyone, but no one acknowledged me.

Fixed my food, felt like a fool.

Still no one said, "Good morning," or even, "How do you do."

Sat down and begin to eat.

Turned on the TV, and what did I see?

A report came.

Didn't catch the name

Of the person they said

Died in that tragic scene.

So much pain.

What does this mean?

Why do I feel so connected to that tragic scene?

Thank you, Lord, for waking me up this morning.

With tears in their eyes of the tragedy,

My family screamed out loud, "How could this be?"

The phone rang; they started to scream.

Why are they constantly mentioning my name?

My name was mentioned, and I wondered,

Why are they pleading to the Lord for my life?

Please, please, can someone explain?

What is going on? What does this all mean?

I heard a voice in reply.

"Good morning, my child, I will explain

The events that took place before this scene.

I knocked on your door many times before,

But you simply refused; and you always ignored.

I am the Lord; there is no one above me.

You always turned and strayed away,

Never establishing a relationship that would forever stay.

You denied my mighty name,

Saying all gods are the same,

Not knowing about the power I maintain.

"Your friends tried to tell you what Christ can do,

But you pushed them away, never beginning your pursuit

Of a relationship that would always last

With a Father who forgives you for your sins of the past.

"This is something I am sorry to say

You will not wake up on this day."

Remarks

We all have been given a chance at life; how we live it is up to us, a freedom of choice.

At the end of our lives, the Bible says we have to account for how we lived it.

Live for God. Nothing to lose, but so much to gain.

What kind of deal is it to get everything you want but lose yourself? (Matthew 16:26)

Lost Identity

———❦❦❦———

How, then, can they call on the one they have not believed in? And how can they believe in the one of whom they have not heard? And how can they hear without someone preaching to them?

—Romans 10:14 (NIV)

Do you see what I see?

Do you see what is happening all around you and me?

Do you see all these calamities?

What should we do to help our society?

Should we not stand as one

To protect our land, to put into practice

The will and purpose of the Master's plans?

The Bible clearly says what we should do,

So why are we afraid to go out and pursue

A life of tranquility, not of fame and gain,

But where we live and serve the Lord's mighty name?

As a church we have become afraid

Of the people in the world and their wicked ways.

We were chosen to help bring them through,

So why are we sitting here as if we don't know what to do?

Our church is a safe place, encouraging each other day after day.

So what happens to the brother man

Who stands outside with tears in his eyes,

Not knowing if he is going to live to see another blue sky?

Or that lady with those five kids who is ready

To take her life because she is tired of living like this,

No food to eat, selling her body on the streets

Just to provide for her family, who seems to have no destiny?

We pray for him and her every day.

But did we go talk to them, letting them know it can—will—be OK?

Did we inform them about the Lord, that he has the power to restore?

Did we do our best to guide them through?

Or did we leave them alone to see what they would do?

The Lord will not be pleased with how we handled his kings and queens,

Not taking them by the hands and leading them to the Promised Land,

And not educating them about his big master plan.

We didn't deliver them from lives of sin,

Allowing them to find peace and joy deep within.

Living a life that they can see a

Future, a tomorrow for them and their families.

Let's get up from our secure place,

Stand, and with faith declare with his blood that it will all be OK.

Let us go preach and teach in the land,

And lead the lost to the promised plans.

Not Crippled

Therefore, if anyone is in Christ, he is a
new creation; old things have passed away;
behold, all things are become new.

—2 Corinthians 5:17

I was crippled all the days of my life.
Could not move to do what was supposed to be right.
I was standing in quicksand,
Sinking like a dead man,
Not understanding the will and purpose
Of the Master's plan.

My life was built on negative speech.
This was heard over and over
And caused me to think,
Is this who I am destined to be?

A nobody in society, with no hope or dreams.
These were some words that tightened my chains:
"A dog would not even be your friend."
"You are a loser; you could never ever win."
"You are a fool to believe
That I would ever be your queen."
"You dummy, please stop getting up from those dreams."
"You are beneath me and will never amount to anything."
"So what makes you so special, Mr. Wannabe?"

A child of God blessed in so many ways
Will never look back at those days.
The strength that has been placed inside me
Has helped me break the chains of my infirmities.
A cripple is what I used to be, but with one touch,
My body, soul, and mind have been set free.

I am above and not beneath,

Now pushing through life,

Fulfilling God's plans and my destiny.

Let me ask you a question.

What did you dream of becoming when you were younger?

What happened along the way that caused you to stop moving forward?

Was it negative words people said to you? Was it how people treated you? Was it lack of confidence? Finances? Support? Knowledge, etc.?

No matter the answer, let me encourage you.

It's not too late to accomplish it.

Put those negative thoughts and words aside, and go for what the Lord has placed in your heart.

You have been filled with the ability to overcome any situation.

Fill yourself with talents and the belief that you are able to do anything you put your mind to.

You are well connected to individuals who are equipped to help you along the way.

Most of all, our heavenly Father has the power to see to it that you succeed.

Being confident of this very thing, that He who has begun a good work in you will complete it until the day of Jesus Christ. (Philippians1:6)

Our Men

I will instruct you and teach you in the way you should go; I will counsel you with my loving eye on you.

—Psalm 32:8 (NIV)

My eyes were closed to what was in front of me—
"gentleman," "respectful," "honest," "visionary,"
"provider," "protector," "hard worker," but most of all "loving."
These used to be some words to describe our men,
Those who were guided by old folks
With God's blueprints plans.
They were taught at an early age
Not to depart from the godly ways.
But somehow things changed.
Now look at men today.
Who is to blame?

"Drug dealers," "pedophiles" "abusers," "drug addicts," "criminals"—
just a few new names that the young men have claimed.
Who is to blame?

Old folks tried to protect them from becoming slaves.
Somewhere down the line, their efforts failed.
"Slave? What do you mean?"
I am glad you asked.
Slave to the enemy who has changed the past
So their futures can look like shattered glass.
Who is to blame?

There's that question again.
I have a better question:
How can our men change and stand up in order to win?

Let us not look to cast the blame,

But look to God for the solution to change.

Our men can be saved.

It begins with us reintroducing them to godly ways.

Do they know they are better than what people say they are?

Do they know they can do all things through Christ, who strengthens them?

Do they know their sins have been forgiven?

Do they know they have a chance for better futures?

Do they know God can restore them?

Let us pray and ask God to show men the way.

While the words we pray strengthen them day by day,

We will have to pray for wisdom and for strength

Because this is a new battle we must win.

Let us navigate through the battlefield

Knowing that the Lord is our armor and shield.

Let us pray for our nation, and

Be careful of the blames we entertain.

We will look to make a change

That our men won't stay the same.

Shaken Faith

In peace I will lie down and sleep, for you
alone, Lord, make me dwell in safety.

—Psalm 4:8 (AMP)

Father, can you help me?
The pressures of this world seem so great.
They have really taken a toll on my faith.
My faith was shaken, to my surprise,
Simply because of the events
That took place in my life.

My mother, who was always there for me,
Died a tragic death right in front of me.
A stray bullet from a nearby fight
Took my mom's life on that Saturday night.
How could this be?
A holy woman to a tee,
She did everything she could to live to keep the peace.

Father, can you help me to understand?
Is this a part of your big master plan?

My sister, she was so sweet,
Did what she could to help the community.
Eight months pregnant and engaged,
So excited for her big wedding day.
Father, help me to understand why
Did her car crash into that telephone line?

My faith is being shaken in so many ways.
Another tragedy took place in the last couple of days.

I came home early, and to my surprise,
My wife was entertaining another guy.
With so much pain inside my heart,
I packed my things and headed for a new start.
I cried out, "Father, Father, help me please.
My mind is going places I don't want to be."

A voice replied,
"Read about Job's life, and you will understand me.
I am taking you to a place
Where you will have to trust in me.
Have faith, my child.
I know where you should be.
You have been faithful in all that you do.
There is so much I have planned for you.
You are my special child, this I can't ignore.
The things that were done to you
I knew you could endure.
Through all your pain and misery,
Not once did you curse my mighty name.

With strength and faith placed inside you,

Everyone will see what the Lord is capable of doing through you."

Shaken Faith: A Message

First, a famine forces her family to migrate to a strange country, leaving friends and family behind. Then her friend, her protector, her lover, her dear husband dies. Just when she begins to heal from this painful loss, her firstborn son dies just like that, without warning. Then her second son dies. Her life is like a soup of nothingness. Whatever is beating inside her chest is nothing but a remnant of what used to be a heart. Empty, void, humiliated, stripped of her life, her joy, she returns home. But in this dark chain of events, Ruth was there (her daughter-in-law) holding Naomi as she Naomi returns home. Ruth follows, leaving friends and family behind. They march into their best lives yet. Read about it in the book of Ruth.

Something Is Missing

Instead of your shame you will receive a double portion, and instead of disgrace you will rejoice in your inheritance. And so you will inherit a double portion in your land, and everlasting joy will be yours.

—Isaiah 61:7 (NIV)

There has been something missing in my life.
Couldn't put a finger on it to make it feel right.
But whatever it is, I will achieve.
I will pursue it with all my means.

What is missing? Should I ask?
Is it money? A fancy home? An expensive car?
Or is it just to live life grand, like a movie star?

What am I missing?
And why can't I see
That what I have accomplished in life is just vanity?
I pursued big things
Thinking I could live life like the queen,
But later I realized I was
Being set up by the enemy's big schemes.
The things I was pursuing had no value at all.
But I stayed chasing just to fill one big void: contentment.

Honestly,
A foundation was laid at a tender young age,
Learning about God
And how to live in the world he has made.
I understood everything that I was supposed to do.
But it didn't feel right, so I began a material pursuit,
Living by the world's system and falling into Satan's traps.
My life stopped advancing because I was on the wrong track.

Encouraging Words

Friend, have you ever felt empty despite partying, drinking, smoking, having sex, hanging out with friends, and so on? Just empty. No matter what you did, something felt missing.

In the Bible, John 4:1–42 speaks about Jesus's encounter with a Samaritan woman. In that culture, Jews were not supposed to associate with a Samaritan. Even worse, a Samaritan woman. She lived with married men who were not her husband. I believe she wanted to feel love, protected, had a sense of longing, and so on. But whatever the reason, she wasn't content because it was repeatedly done. Jesus broke the rules by having a conversation with her. He knows exactly what we need and how and when we need something in our lives. In this case, he offered the woman a way to have joy, peace, forgiveness, and so on.

> But whomever drinks the water I give them will never thirst. Indeed, the water I give them will become in them a spring of water welling up to eternal life. (John 4:14 NIV)

Long story short, the Samaritan woman's emptiness, as well of some of the village people's lives, were filled and put on the right track when they accepted Jesus into their hearts. He alone can fill the void and emptiness.

Ecclesiastes 3:11 (AMP) tells us, "He has also planted eternity in man's heart ... God alone can satisfy."

The Touch

Come to me, all you who are weary and burdened,
and I will give you rest. Take my yoke upon you
and learn from me, for I am gentle and humble
in heart, and you will find rest for your souls.
For my yoke is easy and my burden is light.

—Matthew 11:28–30 (NIV)

The touch, the touch, how I remember those days.

Never to look back on how it destroyed me along the way.

A touch that led me down a road with no control.

My world was based on the touch's hold.

My life fell apart from the very start

With a grip that tore straight through my heart.

Exposed too early to an impure touch

That shattered my innocence like a tidal wave rush.

My parents did not know what was going on.

If they did, their lives would be gone.

That was a promise from the touch.

If I ever spoke,

There would be ashes to ashes, and

My parents would lie six feet in the dust.

My mind was a mess; I didn't realize

The situation made me experience some serious hard times.

Depression, low self-esteem, and suicidal thoughts

Came with the pain of the innocence I had lost.

The touch made me feel dirty, nasty, unwanted,

Frustrated in my heart.

I began seeking a brand-new start.

The reason I mentioned I remember those days

Is because I am healed in such a glorious way.

Church is what a friend said to me.

Sunday afternoon, around three.

I had made up my mind
To attend that day.
When the pastor opened his mouth and began to speak,
A sense of peace overcame me.

The woman he spoke about did what she can
To touch the hem of the garment of the Holy Man.
Her life had been one big mess.
For twelve long years she was carrying a heavy stress.
Being removed from society and her family
Made her more determined to be healed, to rejoin her community.
She made me realize I could have a beautiful life
If I got to know God, he would make my wrongs right.

The real touch I was destined to obtain
I have received through Jesus's mighty name.
I no longer carry that molestation pain.
My new life I now know has been rearranged.
Jesus has touched me.

You Built Me

---✦✦✦---

Neither do people pour new wine into old wineskins.
If they do, the skins will burst; the wine will run out
and the wineskins will be ruined. No, they pour new
wine into new wineskins, and both are preserved.

—Matthew 9:17 (NIV)

You built me with the hard words you would say:
"You are a dummy and always going to be this way."
You built me with slaps and spit in my face,
Built a person with low self-esteem traits.

Something I felt growing inside me.
It was the goodness becoming paralyzed.
What have those words done to me?

Being mistreated is a thing of the past.
The monster they have sown is released at last.
They will pay for what they did to me,
Treating me like garbage, tossing me in the streets,
The pains of life that were dealt to me.
And they said there is a God: How could there be?

God, if you are there, then why me?
How come I don't have a sense of peace inside me?
There is no joy in my heart because it has been torn so many times apart.
I have been abused, misused, and my mind is so confused.
I heard about what you can do.
So my question is, Lord, where are you?

Just so I no longer have to live like this—
In fear, disappointment, neglect, low self-esteem—
Just a few things I entertained
Because of the negative names I have gained.
Who is to blame?
The people in society who have mocked me?

The family members who never supported me?
Or simply the bad choices I made along the way
And getting caught up in situations day after day?

Wow! I never saw it before.
I had opened and walked through so many bad doors.
The choices I made positioned me in this phase.
Oh, God, how do I get out of this maze?

"Stand and confess,"
The man of God said to me.
"Stand and confess," confess what?
What they have said to me?
That caused me to think that this is who I am going to be, "a nobody."
Confess what?
That I allowed their words to define and build me,
Or the fact that I don't see my future becoming a reality?

So what is it that I am to confess?
Confess your sins that are rooted deep within
So the Lord can build you with a new wineskin.
'Cause if he does it with the old you,
It will be ruined, and everything will spill out of you.

Stop holding on to the hurts and the pains.
Let them go so you can begin to change.
You had asked if there is a God.
The answer is yes, yes of course.

He has seen and heard all your pains.
Now these are the new things he wants you to entertain.

You were made in his image,
So you could never be
Garbage tossed out in the streets.
You are a king or queen, destined to do great things,
So the enemy will try and stop what God has ordained.

I urge you to open your heart so you can receive
The new blueprint God has rearranged.
Out with the old, and in with the new.
There is so much he has in store for you.
You are above the negative words people speak
So you will never be beneath anyone's feet.
If you stay focused and faithful to the Lord,
He will always make sure that you are secured.

Lord, forgive me for all my sins.
I ask that you come into my life as Lord and Savior.
Cleanse me of all unrighteousness.
I boldly confess all my sins that were deeply rooted within
So you, oh, Lord, can rebuild me with a new wineskin.

My life is built on the promises of God.
My foundation will now be planted in the Lord.
Blessings and favors will go before me
While the light of the Lord shines through me.
Peace of mind I have gained.

I will speak boldly about the Lord's mighty name.

Unspeakable joy has touched my heart.

This is the moment that will never depart.

I will speak those things that are true.

The Lord has built me. What about you?

You Built Me: A Message

David was a simple young man. His father saw him as the baby of the family. His older brothers, who were much taller, only saw him as the little shepherd, not destined to be anything else or more. Goliath saw a puny boy, nothing to be afraid of. Saul saw a boy marching to his death. But God, God saw King David—the great king, his friend, a man after his own heart. The ancestor of Jesus. Read about it in 1 Samuel 16–30.

A Reminder

In life we have all been called by some harsh names that broke our spirits, confidence, and even our emotions. Whether it's at school, on the job, on the playground, or at home, or by friends, families, or strangers, those words have played over and over in our minds, making us believe those things that were not true.

I am here to let you know those negative words are *not* you. They were the enemy's deceptions to stop you from becoming victorious, stop you from encouraging others, and stop you from receiving your blessings. On the bright side, once you get to know the truth about yourself, you will learn that what's inside you can't be stopped simply because:

You are created in God's image and likeness.

You were designed for greatness.

You were created to be a powerful leader.

A Prayer to Break Negativity

Father, I declare that every negative word that has defined me most of my life is broken and uprooted by the power of the blood. I am walking with a new mindset, with a positive attitude, knowing that all my situations have been turned around in my favor. I declare that all my dormant abilities and talents are now activated in Jesus's name. I will have no more lack, no more mind battles. I can now see myself as Mr./Ms. Unstoppable. In Jesus's name. Amen.

Conclusion

I truly thank God for leading me back home to the Bahamas. While living in Montreal, God and Jesus honestly were not a part of my life despite learning about the Bible principles and values from my mom (Geneva Lafleur) and grandmother (Althea "Tita" Gibson) at a young age. Their teachings were planted in me but not often used.

I lived a carefree, reckless, and dangerous life; I even went as far as getting arrested for attempted murder.

Then one day, due to intense pressure and situations, I was prompted to move back to the Bahamas.

I will say this, "God has a purpose and a plan for all our lives if we allow him to work his will in us."

To my kids, Daddy may not always be around to see you develop into who God has designed you to become. But I am blessed to have you in my life, and I place you all in God's hands. Ephrahti, Astrid, Jamal, LeChawn, Edwin, and Abigail, may the Lord continue to guide you on your journey of life.

I thank God for blessing me with a good family, especially a good wife, Nicole, who sees the potential that has been placed in me and is my personal cheerleader. And to my sister, Ginger, who was always in my corner. May the Lord continue to bless you all and supply all your needs.

I cannot forget Jovie and Leslie, my other two cheerleaders, who have been a big help in me completing my book and their help in taking care of my Booboo. Big thanks.

To all my friends and family who have encouraged me to continue pushing, thank you all.

Let's not give up on life because we may have had some bad breaks. Shake it off and realize that there are so many opportunities just waiting to give us a new perspective. Let us take off the blindfold and see the beauty and wonders that were prepared for us. Enjoy life.

"There are no limitations just Possibilities." By Ephrom Lafleur

Printed in the United States
By Bookmasters